THE
LITTLE
YEARS

by John Mighton

Playwrights Canada Press
Toronto • Canada

The Little Years © Copyright 1995 John Mighton
Playwrights Canada Press 54 Wolseley St., 2nd fl.,
Toronto, Ontario CANADA M5T 1A5
Tel: (416) 703-0201 Fax: (416) 703-0059
e-mail: cdplays@interlog.com
http://www.puc.ca

Playwrights Canada Press operates with the generous assistance of
The Canada Council for the Arts - Writing and Publishing Section,
and the Ontario Arts Council.

*Cover painting, "Royal Crown", by Sunjeat Chohan, Winnipeg,
produced at the Studio Programs Wing of the Winnipeg Art Gallery.*

Canadian Cataloguing in Publication Data
John Mighton, 1957 —
          The little years
A play
ISBN 0-88754-548-3
I. Title.
PS8576.I29L58 1996   C812'.54 C96-931223-7
PR9199.3.M55L58 1996

First edition: August, 1996. Second printing: May, 1998.
Printed and bound in Winnipeg, Manitoba, Canada.

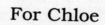

For Chloe

The author would like to thank Pia Kleber and Diane Cave for encouraging him to write the play and for ensuring it was produced in the face of cutbacks to the Why Theatre Conference. He would also like to thank Ji Bai for conversations that inspired the play.

— *John Mighton*

John Mighton lectured in Philosophy at McMaster
University and is presently completing a Ph.D. in
Mathematics at the University of Toronto. His plays, which
include *Scientific Americans, Possible Worlds, A Short
History of Night*, and *Body and Soul*, have been performed
across Canada as well as in Europe and the United States
and have won several national awards including a Governor
General's Literary Award for Drama for the Playwrights
Canada Press publication of *Possible Worlds & A Short
History of Night*..

A man's life includes much that does not take place within the boundaries of his body and his mind, and what happens to him can include much that does not take place within the boundaries of his life.

—*Thomas Nagel*

The Little Years premiered at Theatre Passe Muraille, Toronto, November, 1995, as part of the Why Theatre Conference, with the following cast, in order of appearance:

ALICE	*Anne Anglin*
YOUNG KATE / TANYA	*Kristen Thomson*
MARY	*Melissa Berney*
NORMAN	*Adam Nashman*
MR. CASTLE / ROGER / MR. YORK	*R.H. Thomson*
GRACE	*Fiona Highet*
KATE	*Maggie Huculak*

Directed by Herbert Olschok.
Set and costume design by Olaf Altman.
Lighting design by Peter Freund.
Stage manager — Cheryl Francis.
Assistant stage manager — Melissa Berney.
Original music and sound design by Brad Hilliker.

CHARACTERS

ALICE   William's mother

KATE   His sister.

GRACE   His wife.

TANYA   His daughter.

ROGER   His friend.

KATE should be played by two actors, one younger (Scenes i and ii). The younger actor should double Tanya in Act II. We should have the impression of seeing a way that Kate's life might have gone.

The various male roles may be doubled by the actor playing ROGER (although it would be preferable to have a different actor play the mute boy in Act I.)

Anne Anglin (l), Maggie Huculak (c), Fiona Highet (r) in the 1995 Theatre Passe Muraille production.
— photo by Michael Cooper

Act I, Scene 1

1950. ALICE stands in her garden. Her daughter KATE sits nearby, an open notebook beside her. We hear the wind in the trees.

ALICE   (*calling*) William!

         Pause.

         William!

         She looks at her watch, then at her daughter.

         What are you thinking about?

KATE   My childhood.

ALICE   What about it?

KATE   I wish I could live it over.

ALICE   You're only thirteen.

KATE   I'll never be six again.

ALICE   You're a little young to be regretting your life.

KATE   I stupidly missed so many opportunities. A person can only be truly happy as a child. And I wasn't.

ALICE   Why weren't you happy? You had everything. I spoiled you.

Pause.

ALICE   William!

KATE   If you'd stop calling him, he'd come home.

ALICE   He's going to be late for the ceremony .... are you coming?

KATE   No.

ALICE   You'd win prizes too if you'd put your mind to it.

Pause.

ALICE   What are you doing?

KATE   Listening.

ALICE   To what?

KATE   The wind.

Pause.

ALICE   I've often wondered what you do all day. When you're not at school.

KATE   Time goes by itself.

We hear the wind in the trees.

If you listen sometimes you can hear it.

Pause.

Recently they found out the year is getting longer. Half a second each century.

Pause.

KATE   When you measure time you pick some recurring phenomena. Then you make a leap of faith. You assume it always gives intervals of the same length. But there's no way of knowing for sure. For all we know time could be speeding up or slowing down right now.

Long pause. We hear the wind.

ALICE   Where'd you learn that? At school?

KATE   I never learned anything at school.

ALICE   When I was your age I didn't talk back to my teachers.

KATE   I don't talk back. I just don't answer them.

ALICE   I don't know what you're trying to prove. Your father used to say. "There's only one person I want to be admired by — and that's me."

We hear wind chimes.

People will see his life differently after today. They'll say "That's Homer Wilson's son." They'll know what kind of a father he was.

Pause.

One day you'll have your own children. You'll know what it's like to have hopes for them. Even if they don't understand those hopes. You'll still have them.

Pause.

There's a dance at the church on Friday .... there'll be a lot of nice young men there. Why don't you go with Mary?

KATE   We're not friends anymore.

ALICE   Why not?

      Pause.

Your brother knows how to make people like him.
He's always had the most wonderful sense of humour.

KATE   Did you hear the one about the lady who's stopped for
speeding? The cop says "You were going sixty miles
an hour." And she says "That's impossible. I was
only travelling seven minutes."

      Pause.

ALICE   What's funny about that?

      She looks at her watch.

It's not like your brother to be late. He's usually more
considerate.

      Pause.

Your father used to say "Be as polite to your friends
as you are to yourself."

KATE   How can you be polite to yourself?

ALICE   You know what I mean.

      Pause.

This would have been the proudest day of his life.

KATE   Why do we remember the past and not the future?

      Pause.

ALICE   If you want to go to the dance on Friday, I'll drive you.

>   *Pause.*

>   Are you coming to the ceremony?

>   *Pause.*

>   It would be nice to have the whole family there.

>   *We hear wind chimes.*

>   Please .... for your father.

KATE   He's dead.

***

Scene 2

KATE stands alone in the dark. Fifties music plays. MARY approaches.

MARY   Kate.

KATE   I thought you weren't speaking to me.

MARY   There's someone who wants to dance with you.

KATE   Who?

MARY   That boy over there.

KATE   (*looking at him*) Why doesn't he ask me?

MARY   He's mute.

KATE   (*pausing*) No .... I can't.

MARY   He's very nice.

KATE   Is he a friend of yours?

MARY   Yes.

She motions the boy over.

KATE   Mary! Stop!

The boy approaches.

MARY   This is my friend Kate. This is Norman.

NORMAN nods.

MARY   I guess I'll leave you two alone.

              MARY exits. KATE and NORMAN look at
              each other.

KATE   Hi. I'm Kate.

              Pause.

              I guess you're Mary's friend.

              He nods.

              How long .... I mean, have you known Mary long?

              He nods "Yes."

              Do you go to school around here?

              He nods "No."

              Somewhere else?

              He nods "Yes."

              Do you want to dance?

              They start to dance.

              I don't know what Mary's told you about me. She's
              one of my only friends. But lately we haven't been
              getting along too well.

              Pause.

              My mother made me come to this dance.

              Pause.

              Do you have any interest in the sciences?

He nods "Yes."

KATE   Lately I've been reading about the Michelson-Morley experiment. Have you heard about it?

He nods "No."

A hundred years ago they showed that light always travels at the same speed, regardless of the motion of the earth. Once you accept that you have to abandon absolute time and space. Space contracts and time slows down as you move faster.

Pause.

Have you ever been in love?

Pause.

I have.

Pause.

When you walk down the street, it's like you're falling in love over and over. It's the same feeling you get when you hold a baby. Or when you're at the top of a swing about to fall back.

Pause.

You have the most noble face .... It feels good to be near you.

Pause.

Maybe I could learn to talk to you. Could you teach me to sign?

They kiss. The music ends.

KATE   I guess it's over ... that was wonderful. You're a beautiful dancer.

NORMAN   Thanks.

> *He walks away smiling. KATE throws her glass after him.*

***

Scene 3

*ALICE sits across from MR. CASTLE, the
principal of KATE's school.*

CASTLE   You must be very proud of him.

ALICE   I am.

CASTLE   No one from Sir John A. MacDonald has ever been
invited to the Spelling Olympiad.

ALICE   Your coaching sessions made all the difference.

CASTLE   I do what I can.

Pause.

ALICE   I don't suppose you called to talk about William.

CASTLE   No.

ALICE   She doesn't mean to fight. The other children torment
her.

CASTLE   That's not why I asked you here.

ALICE   Oh.

Pause.

CASTLE   The world is changing.

Pause.

ALICE   Is it?

CASTLE   Even as we speak.

Pause.

The other day I dropped in on Mrs. Field's English class. I asked the children to write an essay about the future — about what year they'd like to come back in and what things would be like then. The last half of the century is going to be very different from the first. I'm trying to prepare the children. This is what she wrote (*reading*) "Most people would like to come back after they die. I'd like to come back before I was born — so I could see what the world was like before I came into it. I've always felt things must have been fundamentally different, that something terrible happened when I was born." The essay rambles on in that way. She made no attempt to follow my guidelines. All her work lately has shown a similar self absorption. She thinks all the students and teachers are against her. I've given this a great deal of thought. I believe she would be happier at a vocational school.

ALICE   A vocational school?

CASTLE   Yes.

ALICE   But she's so bright.

CASTLE   This is nineteen-fifty, Alice. Your daughter is very rigid in her thinking. I don't like to use the word paranoid. She's not going to adapt to the coming changes unless she has a vocation.

ALICE   She wants to be a scientist. She's obsessed with time.

CASTLE   Her marks are very poor.

ALICE   Maybe I could get her to work harder.

CASTLE   We've found that girls don't generally succeed in the
                sciences. They don't have the right spatial skills.
                They can't rotate three dimensional objects in their
                heads.

ALICE   They can't?

CASTLE   No.

                        *ALICE tries to rotate a three dimensional
                        object in her head.*

ALICE   Are you certain about that?

CASTLE   Absolutely.

ALICE   And do they do a lot of that in the sciences?

CASTLE   What?

ALICE   Rotating objects.

CASTLE   Oh, yes.

                        Pause.

                I know this is hard for you. Especially as your son is
                so gifted. But not all children can perform at the same
                level. Some people are born to do great things. And
                others, like you and I, were sent here to help them
                realize their promise.

                        Pause.

ALICE   Have you ever been married?

CASTLE   No.

ALICE   It's hard. Being alone.

CASTLE   I have my work. When I get a student like your son it
         makes it all worthwhile.

ALICE   You're a good man. But under-appreciated.

CASTLE   Only God knows what a person is really like. Only
         God sees your innermost thoughts. "The Lord is my
         light and my salvation; whom shall I fear? The Lord
         is the strength of my life; of whom shall I be afraid?"

         Pause.

         I talked to the principal at Northern Tech. She can
         start there Monday.

ALICE   Alright.

                         ***

Scene 4

Twenty years later. GRACE, WILLIAM's wife, stands with ALICE.

GRACE You must be very proud of him.

ALICE Sometimes I say to myself "Is that really my son they're writing those things about?" (*reading as she flips through some papers*) "...Stunning verbal energy and intelligence"... "Poems by which future generations will seek to know us." This one's my favourite. "Others seem to fade away into triviality."

GRACE Did you ever think he'd be this successful?

ALICE Oh, yes.

Pause.

When he first started writing I used to help him with his work. I told him, "Things are going to be very different in the last half of this century. If you want your poems to last, don't use words whose meanings are going to change — otherwise no one will understand you in ten years. Verbs like "breathing" and "moving" are good. And nouns like "head" and "water". In the future people aren't going to have as much time to read. So don't use words they'll have to look up in the dictionary.

GRACE (*looking through the reviews*) Did you save any bad reviews?

KATE enters.

ALICE   I wasn't going to. But William said if I was going to
             save any I should save them all. He never takes them
             personally or gets angry. Even with the people who
             criticize him.

KATE   Oh, no — he's far too conceited for that. He just feels
             sorry for them.

KATE exits.

ALICE   Her usual cheery self. She lost her job yesterday.

GRACE   Was she laid off?

ALICE   Fired.

GRACE   Why didn't she go on in school?

ALICE   Ask her.

*KATE enters with a box and sets it on the
table.*

KATE   I'm going to have to store some things here. I don't
             have room in my apartment. It's very small.

GRACE   This is still your home, Kate. William and I would
             be happy to have you live here.

KATE   I'll be better on my own. (*looking at her mother*) I
             should have moved out years ago.

ALICE   You would have had to hold a job for more than two
             months.

GRACE looks into one of the boxes.

GRACE   What are these?

KATE   My notebooks.

GRACE   (*opening a book*) Do you write?

KATE   (*taking the book*) For myself.

GRACE   What kind of things do you write about?

KATE   Time.

                       Pause.

GRACE   Just time?

KATE   Space.

                       Pause.

KATE   They're inseparable.

GRACE   Why don't you show them to people?

KATE   They're not very interesting.

              KATE picks up the box.

            I'll store them in the basement.

GRACE   Won't you need them?

KATE   I don't write anymore.

                   SHE exits.

GRACE   She's very reserved with me. I don't think she likes me.

ALICE   Don't take it personally. She doesn't like anyone. Her co-workers said she was impossible to get along with. Do you have any friends you could introduce her to?

GRACE	Well... I... I could think about it. What kind of men does she like?
ALICE	Liars.
GRACE	Has she had any long term relationships?
ALICE	Six months, a year.
GRACE	I have one friend .... he's an artist.
ALICE	I don't know what I did wrong.
GRACE	Sometimes it doesn't matter what a parent does.
ALICE	I remember her coming home in tears, the first day of school. The kids were so hard on her.

Pause.

Her father was the only one who could console her.

GRACE	How old was she when he died?
ALICE	Eight.

Pause.

GRACE	You can't blame yourself. She's surrounded by people who love her now. She has to start taking some responsibility for her life. I'd like to get to know her better. I think I could help her.
ALICE	William was such an easy child.

KATE enters.

KATE	Who are you talking about?
ALICE	(*quickly*) William.

KATE   Please don't talk about me behind my back.

ALICE   I've got better things to do.

KATE   Don't!

> *KATE exits. Long pause.*

ALICE   How was your honeymoon?

GRACE   Wonderful. We met so many interesting people. Some nights we would stay up until dawn, talking.

ALICE   William knows how to draw people out.

> *Pause.*

How old is your friend?

GRACE   Thirty seven.

ALICE   Do you think he could stand her?

> *KATE enters carrying two empty boxes.*

(*pointing at a watch on GRACE's wrist*) Is this new?

GRACE   It's from William. There's an inscription.

> *SHE takes the watch off and hands it to ALICE.*

ALICE   (*reading*) "Forever".

> *ALICE examines the watch. Pause.*

How do you wind it?

GRACE   It's new. It takes a battery.

KATE loads some books from a bookshelf into the boxes. ALICE hands the watch to GRACE.

GRACE   Our trip had a great impact on me. Every day we went swimming, or walking in the rain forest. We saw plants the dinosaurs would have eaten. I felt safe, knowing it all existed apart from us. So much beauty — the same, day after day, since the beginning of the world.

Pause.

(*putting on the watch*) We wanted to stay an extra week.

ALICE   Why didn't you?

GRACE   William's book launch.

Pause.

I'd like to help save that beauty.

GRACE looks at one of KATE's books.

Have you ever thought about going back to school?

KATE   At my age?

GRACE   This is nineteen seventy. Lots of people are doing it.

KATE   I don't have any money.

GRACE   William and I could lend you some. There are more opportunities for intelligent women now. You could work at something you believed in.

KATE   I'd never make enough to pay you back.

She exits carrying one of the boxes.

GRACE   She needs to be around positive, open-minded people. Artists, intellectuals, people who can inspire her.

ALICE   I've tried to get her to go to the art gallery, or to a play. I wish you would spend more time with her. She won't listen to me.

KATE enters.

KATE   Who are you talking about?

ALICE   William.

KATE   You can't seem to help it. What do you suppose he's doing right now? Thinking about us?

Pause.

The world just passes him by at a distance. Nothing bad has ever happened to him. And if it did, he wouldn't notice.

KATE exits with a box.

GRACE   I'll invite her to my party.

ALICE   She's running out of time.

***

Scene 5

Seventies music plays. KATE stands alone with a drink in her hand. GRACE enters.

GRACE Kate.

KATE Yes?

GRACE There's someone who wants to meet you.

KATE Who?

GRACE Roger Quinn.

KATE The painter?

GRACE Yes.

KATE Why does he want to meet me?

GRACE I told him all about you.

KATE You mean you asked him to meet me.

GRACE No. He's very interested in meeting you.

KATE Why? Does he want to learn how to type?

GRACE Kate, please ... here he comes. Please try to be nice.

ROGER enters.

Roger, this is my sister-in-law, Kate.

ROGER   It's nice to meet you.

KATE   I admire your work.

ROGER   Thank you.

KATE   Particularly your recent paintings.

ROGER   Yes. I feel I've matured. Although some of my early paintings are more original. What do you do?

KATE   I'm a secretary.

GRACE   Kate is very modest...

KATE   Unemployed.

GRACE   She really...

ROGER   (*picking up a vase*) Who did this?

GRACE   I did.

ROGER   It's very good.

GRACE   Thanks.

ROGER   Do you have any others?

GRACE   No.

ROGER   Why not?

GRACE   That's all I have in me.

ROGER   One vase?

GRACE   Yes.

ROGER   But you have talent. You could be very good.

KATE   So her vase isn't good?

ROGER   Yes, it's good.

KATE   Then why should she produce more?

ROGER   She could vary her style, experiment, make
            discoveries.

GRACE   I'm happy with just one.

ROGER   It's too bad. You could be famous.

GRACE   Is that what you want?

ROGER   I'd like my work to be recognized.

KATE   To outlive you?

ROGER   Yes.

                    KATE laughs.

            What's funny about that?

KATE   Suppose one of your paintings is put on a rocket ship
            and sent to a distant planet. If two years pass in
            rocket ship time, and ten thousand years pass in earth
            time, how long has your painting existed?

ROGER   I don't know.

KATE   Did you know that some infinite sets are larger than
            others?

ROGER   No.

KATE   It's an elementary fact of set theory. If time branches
            you would have more immortality than in linear
            Newtonian time. Infinitely more immortality.

ROGER   I wasn't aware of that.

KATE   And if time is circular then every work of art would be immortal. A hundred years from now we'll have new ideas about time that we can't even imagine now. Did you ever think about that?

ROGER   No.

KATE   Of course not. You're just a stupid artist. You don't know a thing about time. But you spend your life alone, trying to create something that will last forever. How can you waste your life chasing something you don't understand?

       Pause.

ROGER   Yes, I can see your point.

GRACE   Where are you going?

ROGER   To get a drink.

       He exits.

GRACE   Why did you do that?

KATE   He was a condescending asshole.

GRACE   Why can't you just stop? You're the most negative person I know.

KATE   I just can't close my eyes to it.

GRACE   To what?

KATE   The incredible stupidity.

GRACE   Why can't you be more charitable?

KATE   Charity, universal love — that's for privileged people
            like you. How could someone who's been poor or
            abused all their life understand what you're saying?

GRACE   Your life hasn't been that bad.

KATE   All my life people have tried to destroy me.

GRACE   Oh come off it.

KATE   I've tried to give people my love, I've left myself
            wide open, and I've just been used over and over. You
            go on believing that all that matters is thinking good,
            positive thoughts. Go on believing your own
            thoughts are more real than the things people think
            about you. Everything they say is part of your life, as
            real as your skin. I'm sick of living in other peoples'
            mouths.

GRACE   But William and I love you.

KATE   You tolerate me. But I'm starting to drive you crazy.

                        Pause.

            You should go back to your guests.

GRACE   They'll be fine.

KATE   You're missing your own party.

GRACE   Why don't you come in with me? There are some
            other people I'd like you to meet.

KATE   I think I'll go home.

GRACE   It's early.

KATE   I'm a little tired.

Pause.

GRACE   Are you sure?

KATE   Yes.

Pause.

GRACE   What are you doing Friday?

KATE   Nothing.

GRACE   I'll take you out to lunch. Call me tomorrow.

Pause.

Which way are you going?

KATE   Out the back.

GRACE   I'll put on the light.

KATE   I know my way.

Pause.

GRACE   You know I'd do anything to help you Kate.

KATE   I know.

***

Scene 6

Seven years later. ROGER and GRACE are in the living room of GRACE's, formerly ALICE's, house.

ROGER   I had to park down the street. There's a branch across your road.

GRACE   Did anyone see you?

ROGER   You'd have to be insane to be out in this weather.

They kiss on the cheek. GRACE moves away.

GRACE   What are you drinking these days?

ROGER   Scotch.

She pours him a drink.

How's William?

GRACE   Fine.

ROGER   His book is doing well.

GRACE   Yes. He's in England.

ROGER   What's he doing there?

GRACE   Promoting himself.

ROGER   Why didn't you go?

GRACE   Tanya is too young to travel.

                 Pause.

ROGER   How did you like my show?

GRACE   Your paintings have so much depth, so many layers
                 — it's easy to get lost in them. I stood in front of
                 one for fifteen minutes.

ROGER   I'm sorry I couldn't spend much time talking to you.

GRACE   You had too many admirers.

ROGER   I only wanted to talk to you.

                 He moves towards her. She moves away.

                 He's put on weight.

GRACE   Who?

ROGER   William. I saw him on TV. Does he work out?

GRACE   Sometimes.

ROGER   At a club?

GRACE   Yes.

ROGER   Which one?

GRACE   Premiere.

                 Pause.

ROGER   You've made some changes.

GRACE	How long since you were here?
ROGER	Seven years.
GRACE	And now you're famous.
ROGER	Relatively.

Pause.

You won't believe what they write about me now. They call me the Barry Manilow of the painting world.

GRACE	Who's Barry Manilow?
ROGER	A singer.

Pause.

Your place is beautiful.

GRACE	Thanks.
ROGER	Have you done any more sculpture?
GRACE	No.
ROGER	Does William encourage you?
GRACE	Why do you keep asking about my husband?
ROGER	Just curious.
GRACE	This has nothing to do with my husband. He's not here right now. Just us.

Pause.

ROGER	He must not treat you very well.

GRACE	If you say one more thing about my husband I'll kick you out.
ROGER	Alright.

Pause.

How's your sister-in-law?

GRACE	She's not doing very well.
ROGER	Why? What happened?
GRACE	I don't like to talk about her.
ROGER	I won't tell anyone.
GRACE	It's not that.
ROGER	What is it?
GRACE	I know she wouldn't like it.

Pause.

ROGER	Well who can we talk about?
GRACE	We could talk about you.
ROGER	I'd rather not.
GRACE	Why not?
ROGER	Someone told me that's all I do.

Pause.

I'm a bit depressed. I'm having trouble painting.

GRACE	Are you seeing anyone?

ROGER   Karen Cope.

GRACE   I don't know her.

ROGER   She's a model.

GRACE   Oh, yes.

ROGER   It's not serious.

GRACE   Isn't she a little dense?

ROGER   She's actually very intelligent.

                        Pause.

GRACE   My life is totally boring. The only conversations I
               have are with my daughter.

ROGER   How old is she now?

GRACE   One.

                        Pause.

               Sometimes she just points.

                        ROGER kisses GRACE. He starts to
                        unbutton his shirt.

               (*pulling away*) I'm sorry. I can't.

ROGER   Do you find me attractive?

GRACE   It has nothing to do with you. I don't want to hurt
               William.

ROGER   No one will know.

GRACE   We will.

         Pause.

ROGER   You said he doesn't love you any more.

         Pause.

I wouldn't be doing this if I thought it would hurt William.

         Pause.

As you said, this has nothing to do with William, he's...

         A door slams off stage, they freeze.

GRACE   William?

         ROGER quickly buttons his shirt. He sits and looks towards the door, smiling.

William?

         Pause.

Must have been the wind,

ROGER   You said he's in England,

GRACE   He is, promoting himself.

         Pause.

ROGER   Are we going to make love?

GRACE   Do you have a condom?

ROGER   No.

GRACE	There's an all-night drug store on the corner.
ROGER	Alright. I'll be back in a minute.

> *ROGER exits. GRACE looks at her watch,*
> *then pours herself a drink. She takes off her*
> *watch and puts it in a drawer. After several*
> *seconds, she moves towards a chair and sits.*
>
> *Time passes — at least thirty seconds.*

***

Act II, Scene 1

18 years later. A mausoleum.

MR. YORK   Your husband was a writer, wasn't he? Didn't he write a book?

GRACE   Yes.

MR. YORK   A novel?

GRACE   No, he was a poet. He won a number of national awards.

MR. YORK   Really?

Pause.

Did he write a poem about a dog?

GRACE   Not that I'm aware of.

Pause.

MR. YORK   Do you have the urn?

GRACE   Yes.

GRACE takes an urn out of a box and hands it to MR. YORK.

MR. YORK   This urn has dirt on it.

GRACE   He was buried in our backyard. People kept climbing
               the fence — to pay their respects.

MR. YORK   I see.

               He puts the urn on his desk and cleans his
               hands with a handywipe.

               (*handing her a form*) You should read this carefully.
               All the general rules and regulations of
               Commemorative Services apply to the Mausoleum as
               far as the nature of the case permits.

GRACE   I see.

MR. YORK   Compartments are to be opened only by employees of
               Commemorative Services. This applies to both the
               inside sealer and the crypt front.

GRACE   I'm not planning to move him again.

MR. YORK   Commemorative Services appreciates your decision to
               make this his final resting place. (*pause*) One bronze
               material vase not exceeding 12 cm wide by 20 cm
               high by 12 cm deep will be permitted in the lower
               left corner on niches. Samples of the permitted size
               and type of letter for inscription, as well as ceramic
               pictures and bronze attachments and vases are on
               display at the cemetery office.

GRACE   Thank you.

MR. YORK   Vases and flowers placed in vases must not encroach
               on adjoining crypts.

GRACE   Alright.

MR. YORK   No pedestals, urns, candles, vesper lights or articles of a heavy or cumbrous character shall be placed in any part of the mausoleum. (*pause*) These rules have been adopted to protect your interests and the interests of all crypt and niche burial rights holders as a group.

GRACE   Yes, I'm sure they have.

MR. YORK   And to preserve the beauty of the mausoleum and surrounding grounds.

　　　　　　　　Pause.

　　　　　　　　Are you expecting a lot of traffic?

GRACE   Traffic?

MR. YORK   People. Visiting your husband.

GRACE   I'm not sure.

MR. YORK   Do you have the inscription?

GRACE   (*handing him a piece of paper*) Yes.

MR. YORK   Is this one of his poems?

GRACE   Yes.

MR. YORK   There's a word here I'd have to look up. I don't have a dictionary — what does this mean?

GRACE   A shadow — cast by trees.

MR. YORK   I don't think I've ever seen that word.

GRACE   It's not used much anymore. It also means jealousy. Of another's reputation.

MR. YORK   Umbrage.

Pause.

MR. YORK   (*looking at the poem*) I think I'd have to read this over a few times. I don't read much poetry. I don't have time anymore.

> *He puts the poem in a folder on his desk and picks up the urn.*

It's a great honour having your husband here.

Pause.

I can save the crypt beside him if you'd like.

GRACE   Yes. Thank you.

***

Scene 2

ALICE enters, walking with difficulty.
KATE carries a tray with food.

KATE   (*pointing to an invisible table*) Is this alright?

        Pause.

Is this alright.

        Pause.

Not talking today?

        ALICE walks slowly to a table in the
        opposite direction. KATE looks at her
        watch, then puts the tray on the table.
        ALICE shakes salt on her food.

Why don't you try it first? The doctor said you should
cut down on your sodium.

        ALICE tastes her food then shakes more salt
        on it.

Do you still have insomnia?

ALICE   No. But I couldn't sleep last night.

KATE   What?

ALICE   There was some kind of insect in my room. At first I
          thought it was Mrs. MacNamara — talking to me
          through the wall.

KATE   Have you made any friends here?

ALICE   Just her.

                    Pause.

KATE   I'm sorry I couldn't make it on Monday. I've been
          very busy.

ALICE   Have you sold William's manuscripts?

KATE   Not yet.

ALICE   His reputation is in your hands.

KATE   There's a glut right now. No one can afford to
          preserve all the things that are being written.

ALICE   I don't know why he left them to you. You can't even
          look after yourself.

                    She shakes salt on her food.

KATE   What did you do this week?

ALICE   They took us to the art gallery. There's a new show
          there.

KATE   How was it?

ALICE   We got in with a pack of ten-year-olds. Screaming,
          stamping their feet. And they made us walk so far.
          Our group leader kept trying to get me to babysit this
          woman who's ninety eight. She'd say, "You look
          tired, why don't you sit down beside Mrs.
          Freelander?" The third time I caught on. She said,

ALICE   (*continued*) "Sit down." I said, "I don't want to sit
               down." She said, "Alice, sit down!" I made this sound
               at her. (*she makes a clicking sound with her tongue*)

KATE   Did you notice any paintings?

ALICE   I can't see clearly.

KATE   What?

ALICE   If I look hard at something I can see it. It's as if I
               don't care to look at things.

                              Pause.

               There's something I want. But I don't know what it
               is. You know how sometimes you think "Wouldn't it
               be nice to be listening to the radio right now." and
               suddenly you realize you are listening to the radio.

                        She shakes salt on her food.

KATE   Don't you have enough salt, Mother?

                        KATE looks at her watch.

               I have to go. I'll see you next week.

ALICE   There's something I should tell you.

KATE   I'll miss my bus.

ALICE   It's time I prepared you.

KATE   For what?

ALICE   Life.

                              Pause.

KATE   I'm sixty years old.

ALICE   It's not too late. (*pause*) Do you remember when you were young? I used to comb your hair and tell you how beautiful you were?

KATE   Yes.

ALICE   Well you weren't. I lied. I'm sorry. (*pause*) You're an unusual looking woman. Sometimes you can look so pretty and other times you're so homely.

KATE   I'm quite aware of how I look.

ALICE   William was so handsome.

KATE   Why do you say these things to me mother? How did I disappoint you?

ALICE   You should have married that boy who proposed to you in high school. You'd have children now. To take care of you.

Pause.

No one will remember you.

Pause.

KATE   Why aren't you eating your chicken?

ALICE   I'm saving it.

KATE   What for?

ALICE   For my kitty.

KATE   You don't have a kitty.

ALICE   She slept on my television last night. Her purring
               kept me awake.

KATE   They don't allow animals here.

                    Pause. ALICE stares ahead.

               Mother?

                    Pause.

ALICE   Tell William to come and see me. I worry about him.

                         ***

Scene 3

GRACE and ROGER are in GRACE's garden.

ROGER   Do you think a person could change without losing or gaining any characteristics?

GRACE   I suppose if the world changed and the person remained the same they might seem to have changed. Why?

ROGER   I've changed.

GRACE   You don't seem any different.

ROGER   I'm not.

Pause.

ROGER   Am I?

GRACE   No.

Pause.

GRACE   Kate's here.

ROGER   Is she still so opinionated?

GRACE   She's changed.

ROGER   In what way?

GRACE   She's lost that spark she used to have. She's not as quick-witted. Since she got here she's spent most of her time in her room. She's probably there now.

ROGER   I'd like to talk to her.

GRACE   She doesn't say much.

> *GRACE looks at her watch, the one WILLIAM gave her.*

I should start clearing away some of the food.

ROGER   Where's Tanya?

GRACE   Preparing her speech.

ROGER   How many prizes did she win?

GRACE   The physics prize, the mathematics prize, and a prize for scholarship. Plus a medal for track and field.

ROGER   It's too bad William's not here.

> *He takes her hand.*

GRACE   Don't.

ROGER   Why not?

GRACE   I don't know how I feel about you.

ROGER   You would if I was successful.

GRACE   You are successful.

ROGER   They call me the Barry Manilow of the painting world.

GRACE   Is that bad?

ROGER   It is now.

Pause.

I saw the piece on William in *The Times*.

GRACE   (*angry*) William wasn't a person who would write anything "trite" or "precious" . He was the most vital person I've known.

Pause.

ROGER   Did he ever suspect?

GRACE   No.

Pause.

ROGER   How's work?

GRACE   Not good.

ROGER   It must be strange being an environmentalist.

GRACE   Why?

ROGER   Because when you look back on your life you haven't done anything. You've tried to keep things the way they were.

Pause.

GRACE   I told Tanya.

ROGER   Why?

GRACE   I didn't want her to hear it from someone else.

ROGER   But no one knew!

Pause.

ROGER I'm going to feel very awkward around her.

GRACE She understands.

ROGER I just don't want the whole world to know.

GRACE Who's she going to tell?

Pause.

GRACE Are you seeing anyone?

ROGER Mary Dixon.

GRACE Mary?

ROGER Yes.

GRACE She's older than you.

ROGER So?

GRACE Isn't that a problem?

ROGER Are you that superficial?

GRACE No, but you are. You always wanted a young trophy wife. So people would admire you.

ROGER No. I've changed.

GRACE Have you? Or is it just your prospects that have changed?

ROGER What's the difference?

Pause.

ROGER   I heard Kate was institutionalized.

KATE enters.

GRACE   Years ago. She's seeing a psychiatrist now. She has a decent job. She's not as bitter and jealous of everyone. I'm going to try to spend more time with her.

GRACE sees KATE.

KATE   Excuse me.

She turns to leave.

GRACE   Kate. Come and join us.

KATE   I don't want to disturb you.

GRACE   Roger wanted to talk to you.

GRACE stands.

ROGER   Where are you going?

GRACE   I should get back to my guests.

GRACE exits. Pause.

ROGER   I'm Roger.

KATE   I know.

ROGER   We met here twenty seven years ago. June 12. At 7:45 pm.

KATE   Is there some reason you wanted to talk to me?

ROGER   Yes. There is.

Pause.

ROGER	Do you remember what you said to me that day? About time?
KATE	No.
ROGER	You said I didn't know what it was.
KATE	Did I?
ROGER	Yes.

Pause.

KATE	Well, I'm sorry.

Pause.

ROGER	You were right. I spent months thinking about what you said. I couldn't see any point in chasing something I didn't understand. I thought about the whole idea of artistic immortality — it's quite recent — a cultural creation. Artists used to make things anonymously — to glorify rulers or gods. I realized I was only painting to be admired, not because I had any great spiritual thing to say. But I went on painting, even though everything I did seemed forced and artificial. Because I didn't know how to do anything else.

Pause.

These days I can sit in a chair for eight hours, staring at a canvas.

Pause.

I'm not blaming you — but success is a kind of spell. You broke the spell.

Pause. KATE begins to exit.

ROGER   Where are you going?

KATE   To get a drink.

ROGER   No please .... it would have happened one day. I was never a genius. I might have gone through life thinking I was. Now at least I know myself. I have you to thank for that.

                     Pause.

             Do you know how hard it is — to have everything taken away from you?

KATE   I wouldn't know. No one's ever given a damn about what I do.

ROGER   You're lucky! There are some critics I'd like to kill. You never lose the fears and insecurities you had as a kid. All it takes is one bad review in a national paper. It's like being beaten up in the playground — by a million kids!

                     Pause.

             Your brother hasn't fared too well. I read the obituaries. They call me "academic" too. He wasn't a bad writer. Some of his poems have stuck with me.

                     Pause.

             Are you still reading all those books about science?

KATE   Not anymore.

ROGER   Why not?

KATE   I don't like reading popularizations. I never feel I understand what they're saying.

ROGER	Why didn't you go into math then?
KATE	I didn't think I was intelligent enough.
ROGER	But Grace says you were quite precocious.
KATE	If you think you can walk over hot coals you can. It's even easier to convince yourself you can't do something. That's why schools exist.
ROGER	It's not too late. You could go back.
KATE	Once was enough.

Pause.

I retire in five years. I'm trying to hold on to my job — for the benefits. I've been passed over for promotion five times. But I've learned to keep my mouth shut.

ROGER	What happened to us?

Pause.

KATE	You're one of the privileged few.
ROGER	I was. Once.
KATE	No. Even now. You were famous.
ROGER	Once.
KATE	Yes .... for a moment people felt pleasure looking at your work, they stopped thinking about themselves, they believed there was something there .... in the colours, the forms .... that only you could express .... something eternal — for a moment people believed you had something to convey to them .... What more can you ask for?

Pause.

ROGER   I'm not sure how I should take that. Is that supposed to cheer me up?

Pause.

Well it was interesting talking to you, as usual. I suppose I'll be thinking about what you said for another thirty years.

> *He exits. We hear the wind. KATE closes her eyes and listens. TANYA enters.*

TANYA   What are you thinking about?

KATE   My childhood. (*pause*) I used to play under these trees.

Pause.

TANYA   Can I get you anything?

KATE   No thanks.

TANYA   Are you enjoying the party?

KATE   Yes.

TANYA   I'm sorry I haven't spent much time talking to you. I'm a bit preoccupied. I have to make a speech.

KATE   Are you nervous?

TANYA   Yes. Do you have any advice?

KATE   I haven't made many speeches.

TANYA   It's so nice having you here. I hope my room isn't too uncomfortable.

KATE   No .... It used to be mine.

                               Pause.

TANYA   What do you think of Roger?

KATE   Who?

TANYA   The man you were talking to.

KATE   I don't know.

TANYA   My mother had an affair with him.

KATE   How do you know?

TANYA   She told me. (*pause*) He's been teaching me to paint. I think he still likes her. (*pause*) When I leave she'll be alone here.

KATE   Have you chosen a university?

TANYA   I'd like to be close to home. But there are better programs further away.

KATE   What are you taking?

TANYA   Math.

                               Pause.

        I hate having to specialize. Do you think I should take a year off?

KATE   What for?

TANYA   To travel. There are so many things I want to do. A friend of mine wants me to go to India with him.

KATE   I don't know.

Pause.

TANYA   Have you heard of imaginary time?

KATE   What's that?

TANYA   We measure time using real numbers. But if you use
               complex numbers you get a new kind of time. The
               universe is closed, like a sphere, with no
               singularities.

KATE   I'm afraid it's all beyond me.

                         Pause.

               I'm a little tired. I didn't sleep well last night. I may
               leave before the ceremony.

TANYA   I understand.

                         Pause.

KATE   It's hard being away from home. I'm not very good at
               parties. I'm sorry. I'm not sure why your mother
               invited me.

TANYA   I asked her to.

                         Pause.

               I've learned so much from you, Aunt Kate.

KATE   We've never spoken.

TANYA   When I was twelve I found a box of your books in
               the basement. With your diaries. I read them.

                         Pause.

TANYA   You made me think about infinity, the beginning and end of time, things I'd never heard about at school. I saw how vast and mysterious the world is and that I would never run out of things to inspire me. Until then I'd been an average student. You made me believe I could do anything I wanted, as long as I believed in myself.

Pause.

I wish I had more time to talk to you .... Why don't you stay a little longer?

KATE   I can't. I have to be back at work.

TANYA   Do you like your work?

KATE   No.

TANYA   Then why do you do it?

KATE   To stay alive.

TANYA   You should quit.

KATE   It's not that easy.

Pause.

TANYA   There's something I wanted to ask you.

KATE   What's that?

TANYA   What was my father like?

KATE   You know what he was like.

TANYA   You're the only person who knew him his whole life. When he was young, was he happy?

KATE   Yes.

TANYA   Did he have a lot of friends?

             Pause.

KATE   (*slowly, without emotion, as if trying to remember*) We always had kids hanging around the house, from morning until night. And he kept in touch with them over the years. A lot of them were at the funeral. Everyone who met him knew there was something different about him. He was so full of life, so excited about everything. And he could talk to anyone about anything. You see, he really believed that everyone has the potential to be great or interesting. He believed that people are born equal, that we've created a false hierarchy of talent and intelligence, to keep from thinking about death. He hated being famous. He said, "I used to learn things talking to people — now I only hear about myself."

             Pause.

TANYA   This morning I had to get some clothes out of my drawer. I found some pills.

KATE   They were prescribed for me.

             Pause.

They help me sleep.

TANYA   Sometimes I'm so afraid, Aunt Kate.

KATE   Of what?

TANYA   Everyone expects so much from me.

KATE   It doesn't matter what they think. Just do your best.

TANYA   I miss him. I wish he was here.

GRACE enters.

KATE   He is here.

GRACE   We have to go. Do you have your speech?

TANYA   It's in the house.

TANYA exits.

GRACE   It's too bad you can't stay. She worships you.

Pause.

I appreciate your coming.

Pause.

I'm going to have to sell the house. It's too big for one person. What should I do with your books?

KATE   Give them away.

GRACE   And your diaries?

KATE   Burn them.

GRACE   Aren't you being a little dramatic?

KATE   Throw them out.

GRACE   Tanya might like them.

KATE   Fine.

GRACE   They're really very interesting. I could show them to a publisher I know.

KATE   Do what you want.

Pause.

I donated William's manuscripts to a university.

GRACE   Good.

Pause.

I'm going to miss this garden. William and I would
sit here in the evening. Sometimes we'd have friends
over. We'd stay up all night talking. About nothing.

Pause.

GRACE   You don't have to be alone. You could spend more
time with us.

KATE   I've learned a lot from you, Grace. I watch how you
are with people. I appreciate what you've done for me.
But there's something missing that I'll never find. I
had so much to give, so much love.

We hear the wind.

GRACE   You can't see the wind, only what it touches.

Pause.

As I get older, I feel more and more invisible. I can
only see myself in my friends. They're my real body.

Pause.

Sometimes when I'm crossing a room, I can't hear the
separate conversations, only the overall sound. More
and more I listen for that sound.

Pause.

GRACE   Why don't you stay a few more days?

KATE   I can't. My boss is a bitch. She's just waiting for a chance to fire me.

GRACE   Are you coming to the ceremony?

KATE   Yes.

GRACE   (*calling*) Tanya! (*looking at her watch*) We're going to be late.

KATE   Once my brother told me he could hear time passing. He told me you could only hear it when there was no other noise, no traffic or voices. (*GRACE exits*) One night when my parents were asleep, I snuck out into our backyard. I walked to the centre of the garden and stood, with my eyes closed, listening. But all I could hear was the wind moving in the trees. I stood there in the dark and listened to the wind moving in the trees.

               A rough shadow, like one cast by trees at sunset, grows longer and longer until it fills the stage.

               The End.

Other plays by John Mighton
from Playwrights Canada Press

Winner of the Governor General's Literary
Award

Possible Worlds & A Short History of Night
ISBN 0-88754-479-7 / $10.95

Scientific Americans
ISBN 0-88754-488-6 / $10.95